Anne C. Repnow

Some Snowdrops

A Photographic Ramble

With a Foreword by Matt Bishop

Davidia Press

Foreword

For her role as the moderator for the German Facebook group, *Galanthusfreunde*, and as the driving force of the well-established snowdrop event, *Schneeglöckchentage im Luisenpark* at Mannheim, the author's name has become familiar to galanthophiles everywhere. It is, however, through her gorgeous images of choice snowdrops growing in her garden that Anne's love for these flowers is impossible to miss. They have now been brought together, with a few supplementary images from other collectors, into a single volume for all to enjoy.

As someone known to photograph the odd snowdrop, I've long decided on a make-shift studio for this process, where conditions are easily manipulated. One can, therefore, marvel at the quality of the images in Anne's book and the commitment, amid the variables of wind, rain and temperature, required to capture them. Such challenges have tellingly resulted in a lack of really good outside snowdrop close-up photography, common to all the books on the subject.
Until now, that is.

September 2020

Matt Bishop

Left:
Bird bath surrounded by snowdrops at Lyn Miles' Westcroft Garden, UK

Page 04 and 05:
Ancient trees in a sea of snowdrops at Welford Park, UK

Above: Gisela and Horst Maier's garden near Frankfurt, Germany

Page 07: Jörg Lebsa's Garden near Leipzig, Germany

Page 08: Snowdrops sheltering amidst the roots of an ancient beech tree at Brechin Castle, Scotland.

Contents

Introduction

Does the title *Some Snowdrops* seem vaguely familiar to you? It may remind you of the classic book *Some Flowers* by Vita Sackville-West. The intention is the same: it is practically impossible to feature all named snowdrops in one book – there are a mind-blowing number of *Galanthus* cultivars these days and the rate at which they appear (and disappear) is breathtaking. Therefore, I want to share with you the beauty of some snowdrops, though all snowdrops are dear to me. I made a personal choice and selected snowdrops from a range of cultivars I am familiar and feel comfortable with. Some are beloved classics, some are still rare, but all are available – somewhere.

I am no *Galanthus* expert of any standing and there are excellent snowdrop books around with a wealth of information on their cultivation, on species and on botanical background, particularly the invaluable Book *Snowdrops – A Monograph of Cultivated Galanthus* by Matt Bishop, Aaron Davis and John Grimshaw. It would be plain silly to try and match this.

What I felt was missing was a book showcasing images of whole snowdrop plants in a garden setting rather than zooming in on the blooms alone. A book that shows *Galanthus* not as a collectors' item but a flowering plant that gives enormous joy in those months when our gardens are at rest, days are short, the weather is dismal. With this photographic ramble I want to show you how these brave little flowers master the vicissitudes of winter, looking pristine and perfect, each cultivar expressing its distinct character as a garden plant.

Some Snowdrops covers 90 different cultivars, presented in alphabetical order. The short descriptive texts accompanying the photographs reflect personal experience. As part of the snowdrop descriptions I include a little table for each plant giving some indication of its price range, flowering time and vigour. It is a personal view to be taken with a pinch of salt but may be helpful to snowdrop beginners.

Price range: Prices vary from nursery to nursery, country to country and year to year. The price for very expensive snowdrops dwindles over time. Nevertheless, some will never be as cheap as others, their propagation being more of a challenge. Thus, my evaluation depends on my experience at this point in time and should be considered a general indication. In the table, 1 coin indicates a price up to 30 €, 2 coins up to 80 € and 3 coins refer to the staggering range of prices above 80 €.

Flowering time: I am well aware that this varies from year to year and location to location (even within one garden). And – one may wonder – when is a snowdrop in flower? When the flower has dropped from the spathe? When it has opened up? Some snowdrops are in flower for up to 6 weeks! In spite of all these misgivings, this information needed to be included because flowering time is such an important consideration in a garden plant and essential when creating a winter garden or a planting with particular winter interest. In the table, the small time scale helps to put flowering time into perspective.

Vigour: Again this is a matter of personal experience and may vary from location to location. But as a general indication it may be helpful – for example if you are looking for a snowdrop to plant in drifts. In the table, 1 bloom means this snowdrop may be fickle, 2 blooms indicate a normal rate of increase, and 3 blooms stand for an exceptionally vigorous plant.

Snowdrops accompany me in my garden from October to March. They drive away the winter blues and have taught me to look closely in order to appreciate their overwhelming variation. With this book I hope to share my enthusiasm and joy.
And if *Some Snowdrops* finds favour with you and the galanthophile community – who knows? – perhaps there will be a sequel:
More Snowdrops …

Anne

Acknowledgments

It is all Alan Street's fault. He cornered me in Mannheim at the big German snowdrop event „Schneeglöckchentage im Luisenpark" in February 2020 and told me in no uncertain terms that I should publish my Galanthus photos in a book. At first, I felt this would be presumptuous. But when Joe Sharman and Janet Benjafield joined him and reiterated Alan's idea over the next couple of days, I started to think seriously about it. Eventually, when Matt Bishop supported the idea as well, I decided to go for it.

I am tremendously grateful to Alan and Joe for planting the idea of the book. And I cannot thank Matt and Alan enough for reading my texts and providing valuable information. Matt saved me from a number of blunders, pointed out mistakes and advised me on botanical conventions. Thank you for standing by me.

It is not always easy to find out about the origins of particular cultivars. I would not have been able to put together this information without the help of snowdrop friends from all around the world, many of whom also very kindly provided lovely images of some of their favourite plants (see "Contributors"). My sincere thanks go to: Horst and Ingrid Bäuerlein, Janet Benjafield, Ruben Billiet, Mark Brown, Timothy Calkins, Brian Ellis, Hagen Engelmann, Rick Goodenough, Chris Ireland-Jones, Cyril Lafong,

Jörg Lebsa, John Lonsdale, Johan Mens, Ruslan Mishustin, Iris Ney, Calvor Palmateer, Angelina Petrisevac, Jānis Rukšāns, Thomas Seiler, Stephen Shaw, Uwe Stiebritz, Paddy Tobin, and Olivier Vico. My lovely goddaughter Lucy Spoliar and my wonderful son Robin Repnow checked texts and made excellent suggestions – thank you!

A special thank you goes to Iris Ney. She supported my organisation of the event „Schneeglöckchentage im Luisenpark" right from the start and opened a whole new world to me when I accompanied her

on her „Galanthours" to Britain. It was here that I first experienced winter gardens where snowdrops are the icing on the cake, their bright blooms glowing amongst other plants of winter interest. It was very inspiring to visit beautiful parks and private snowdrop gardens and to talk to British galanthophiles. A number of Iris' beautiful photos are included in this book.

Working with publishers is not an unmitigated joy – I know as I worked in the book and journal business for 30 years. So I wasn't shattered when „Some Snowdrops" was rejected by traditional publishers both in Germany and Britain. However, producing an attractive book and distributing it internationally is highly skilled work. The publication of the book you are holding in your hands would have remained a dream were it not for the excellent work of the brilliant publishing consultant Dr. Arne Schäffler and his team at Prinz 5 in Augsburg. I successfully worked with Arne in my previous career and was delighted when he took on this unusual project. I am grateful to him for the excellent advice and input he gave every step of the way. It was a joy to realise this book together.

Zu guter Letzt möchte ich mich bei meinen deutschen Schneeglöckchen-FreundInnen dafür entschuldigen, dass ich dieses Buch – nach reiflicher Überlegung – auf Englisch verfasst habe. Ich hoffe, Ihr seht es mir nach! Die Fotos der verschiedenen Galanthus-Sorten sind ja der wichtigste Teil, der englische Text ist nur die Garnitur – ermöglicht jedoch eine internationale Verbreitung.

Left: An ancient oak amidst snowdrops against the backdrop of the famous lake at Colesbourne Park, GB.
Page 12: Early spring tableau at Dineke Logtenberg's Tuin de Boschhoeve

'Ailwyn'

Price	€ (coin symbol)
Blooming time	Early
Vigour	(two snowdrop symbols)

The tightly and very regularly packed inner segments give the double flower of 'Ailwyn' a very chubby appearance and make it stand out even in cold and dreary weather. The outer segments are pure white and boat-shaped, the inners often bear two light-green dots above the darker green apical V. These "eyes" appear in some years and some locations, in others they are absent. 'Ailwyn' is medium sized and its glaucous leaves show some *elwesii* ancestry. It was found by Richard Nutt at Anglesey Abbey in 1994 and named after Lord Fairhaven.

'Angelina'

Price	 *(two euro symbols)*
Blooming time	Main Season
Vigour	*(two snowdrop symbols)*

Though small in stature, 'Angelina' has beautiful large flowers and the scapes sometimes bend under their weight. Two thirds of the outer segments are covered in a glowing bright green wash, leaving the slightly turned up apex white. The darker green apical mark on the inner segments is deeply divided by the pronounced sinus notch. The prostrate leaves are short when 'Angelina' is in flower. This stunning *Galanthus nivalis* was discovered around the year 2000 by Zlatko Petrisevac in Istria (Croatia) and named by Wolfgang Kletzing for Zlatko's wife.

'Anne of Geierstein'

Price	€
Blooming time	Main Season
Vigour	

The most notable feature of this lovely snowdrop of pleasing shape and smallish stature is the unusually thick texture of the rounded outer segments, a feature ensuring that 'Anne of Geierstein' gives pleasure for a longer time. The leaves are neat and show its *plicatus* and *nivalis* ancestry. Raised by William Thomson in the last years of the 19th century, it was named by Samuel Arnott in the beginning of the 20th century, making 'Anne of Geierstein' one of our oldest snowdrop cultivars.

'Atkinsii'

Price	
Blooming time	Early
Vigour	

There is nothing spectacular about 'Atkinsii', but it is a hybrid snowdrop of great elegance and a superb garden plant. It is a fairly tall snowdrop, and both leaves and scapes are upright. The outer segments are narrowly elliptical and concave. In full bloom they give the flowers a characteristic "triangular" look. The inners are slightly flared and the perfect green heart above the sinus notch is slightly blurred towards the base.

Galanthus 'Atkinsii' originates from the garden of James Atkins and has been available for about 150 years.

'Autumn Snow'

Price	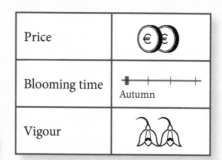
Blooming time	Autumn
Vigour	

Both inner and outer segments of this large-flowered poculiform *Galanthus reginae-olgae* are thickly textured and pure white – usually. Rarely, there is a sliver of green on the inner segments, which are a little shorter than the outers, sometimes retaining a rudimentary sinus notch. 'Autumn Snow' is always one of the first snowdrops to bloom in autumn, at which time the narrow leaves are still below ground. The flowers open up wide in warm sunshine, attracting pollinators. 'Autumn Snow' was selected and named by Patty Peck around 2010.

'Beany'

Price	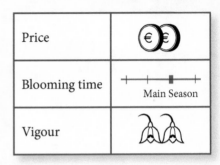
Blooming time	Main Season
Vigour	

With its fat and chunky flowers 'Beany' is undoubtedly one of the finest greentipped *Galanthus elwesii var. monostictus* available. The pointed tips of the large rounded outer segments are marked with a flashy olive-green frayed fan. The sinus notch is small and the big darker green mark above it almost circular. 'Beany' is not a tall plant at flowering but upright and well proportioned. It was discovered at Waltham Place in Berkshire in 2001.

'Bertram Anderson'

Price	€
Blooming time	Main Season
Vigour	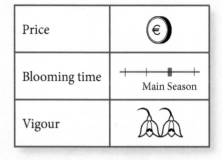

As a member of the hybrid 'Mighty Atom' complex, 'Bertram Anderson' is a large, upright and showy snowdrop with big rounded flowers. It increases well in the garden, where it makes an impression even from a distance. The inner segments have a bold mark above the sinus notch, which blurs slightly towards the ovary. Found by Christopher Brickell in the garden of the late Bertram Anderson, it was named in his honour in 1971.

'Bill Clark'

Price	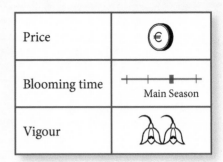
Blooming time	Main Season
Vigour	

In 1987 the warden of Wandlebury Ring, Bill Clark, found this yellow *G. plicatus* in the same location which gave rise to 'Wendy's Gold'. Fittingly, it was later named in his honour. The plicate leaves are a little narrower and the scapes usually a little more upright than in 'Wendy's Gold'. But the most distinguishing feature is the large yellow mark on the inner segments which is well defined and rounded, resembling the backside of a piggy bank.

'Bitter Lemons'

Price	€€
Blooming time	Main Season
Vigour	(snowdrops)

Discovered in the famous copse at Avon Bulbs, close to the spot where 'Midas' was found, the marks on the flaring outer and on the inner segments of this inverse poculiform (pterugiform) hybrid change from a lemony green to a lemony yellow as the flower ages. As in 'Midas', this effect may be more or less pronounced in the flowers of a clump. 'Bitter Lemons' was named by Alan Street and was first offered by Avon Bulbs in 2019.

'Bloomer'

Price	€
Blooming time	Main Season
Vigour	

A seedling of 'Tubby Merlin', 'Bloomer' is one of those snow-drops that look delightful in bud as well as in bloom. Its chartreuse ovary is particularly striking and forms a lovely colour contrast to the neat glaucous leaves of this medium sized and well proportioned plant. The outer segments are rounded, the inners a little frilly along the bottom, indicating some *G. gracilis* in its parentage. The inner segments are entirely marked in green, which is darker close to the sinus notch and towards the base. It was first known as 'Frilly Knickers' at North Green before John Morley gave it the more respectable name 'Bloomer' in the early 1990s.

'Castle Green Dragon'

Price	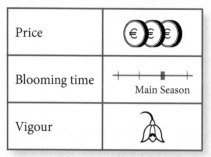
Blooming time	Main Season
Vigour	

The lush, broad leaves, typical of *Galanthus plicatus*, enhance the beautiful virescent flower of this showy snowdrop. Strong green lines cover about three quarters of the broad outer segments, leaving the tip a pure white. The inners are completely marked in green. As in all virescents the green marking on the outer segments shows up best in a (semi-)shady position.

Found by Ian Christie in the grounds of Brechin Castle, its name refers to the dragon depicted on the castle's flag.

'Chameleon'

Price	€€€
Blooming time	Main Season
Vigour	

Aptly named, 'Chameleon' is a colour-change *Galanthus* × *valentinei*. The inner segments of the pleasingly substantial, rounded flowers are marked with a broad heart above the sinus notch. The colour of this mark bleeds out towards the ovary. These markings differ from flower to flower, from year to year and sometimes change as the flower matures. In one clump the inner segment marks may be olive green bleeding to yellow in some flowers, completely yellow or completely green in others. This striking effect is enhanced by the bluish-green, glaucous prostrate leaves. 'Chameleon' was introduced by Richard Bashford in the early 2010s.

'Cicely Hall'

Price	€
Blooming time	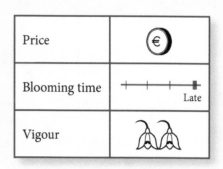 Late
Vigour	

One of several splendid Irish snowdrops, hybrid 'Cicely Hall' may not be elegant, but she is very imposing – tall, with upright, sturdy scapes and equally upright broad, glaucous leaves. The flowers are large, chunky and of excellent substance. The ovary is big and waisted, its dark green colour matching perfectly the solid green of the inner segments. Above the pronounced sinus notch a thin white ribbon runs along the apex and the dark green gets a little lighter close to the base. The outer segments are big, rounded and turned inward. Raised about 1969 by Cicely Hall and her son Robin.

'Cider with Rosie'

Price	€
Blooming time	Main Season
Vigour	

The harmonious combination of lush, shiny green leaves with a well-proportioned inverse poculiform flower makes this *Galanthus woronowii* stand out. The U above the sinus notch of the inner segments, the green "crown" around the apex of the outer segments and the ovary are of a light olive-green colour.

Kevin Minchu, a cider maker from Tewkesbury, discovered this charming snowdrop in a local garden center.

'Cliff Curtis'

Price	€
Blooming time	Main Season
Vigour	

The claws on the pristine rounded outer segments of 'Cliff Curtis' elongate in time, thus showing off the beautifully marked, ridged inner segments of this hybrid snowdrop: two dark green comma-shapes on either side of the sinus notch are complemented by an area of delicate, yellowish-green shading in the middle of the segments. The leaves are neat and upright.

'Cliff Curtis' was raised and named by consensus in 2003.

'Cowhouse Green'

Price	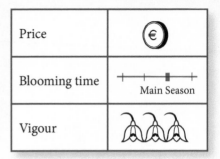 €
Blooming time	—|—|—■—|— Main Season
Vigour	

What is it that makes this snowdrop instantly recognisable? It must be the combination of distinctly marked flowers, long elegantly curved pedicels and tall scapes. The outer flower segments are pointed and marked in apple green. The V towards the apex of the inner segments delicately runs up the segment margins to the base. The special character of this *Galanthus × valentinei* with its neat prostrate leaves is particularly noticable when it is planted on a slope.
'Cowhouse Green' was found and named by Mark Brown in the late 1980s.

'Diggory'

Price	€
Blooming time	Main Season
Vigour	

Everybody loves 'Diggory' – and rightly so! Beautiful glaucous *Galanthus plicatus* leaves combine with large unusual flowers swinging from long nifty pedicels on robust scapes. The outer flower-segments are strongly textured like seersucker material. As they grow and the claws elongate, they balloon out because the edges of the segments do not grow accordingly and the apices curve inwards. The inner segments are almost entirely marked in a light olive green, a pleasing contrast to the leaves. It was found in Norfolk by Rosie Steele and Richard Hobbs in 1993 and named after Rosie's son.

'Ding Dong'

Price	€
Blooming time	Early
Vigour	

The slender flower of 'Ding Dong' is topped by a slightly elongated light olive green ovary. The slim outer segments are pointed and the long claws show up the prettily marked inner segments: The broad U above the sinus notch blurs in a wash towards the base, leaving a narrow lozenge of lighter green in the middle. Short, upright leaves and a habit of producing two flowers per bulb enhance the value of this elegant hybrid as a garden plant.

'Ding Dong' was named (tongue in cheek) by Alan Street and introduced by Avon Bulbs in 2001.

'Dodo Norton'

Price	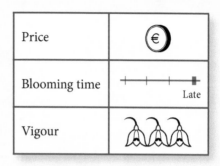 €
Blooming time	Late
Vigour	

Though small in stature, this hybrid snowdrop has large, thickly textured flowers on long pedicels, making it particularly showy when grown on a slope or wall. The outer segments are slightly puckered to give a seersucker effect, the inner segments are boldly marked. The leaves are glaucous and slightly explicative. Found around 1990 in the famous ditch at East Lambrook Manor, 'Dodo Norton' was named after a previous owner in 2000.

'Dumpy Green'

Price	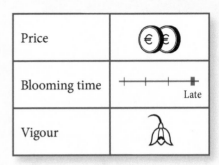 €€
Blooming time	Late
Vigour	

One of the latest snowdrops to appear in the garden, 'Dumpy Green' is taller than the name implies. The glaucous leaves have a blueish tinge and are widely splayed, while the scapes stand upright. The outer segments of the flowers are slightly shouldered and a band of stripy green spreads across the lower half, where the apical edges curve inward. At the base elongated claws ensure a good view of the strongly ridged inner segments. The green V above the sinus notch is flat-angled. 'Dumpy Green' was raised from seed collected by John Morley and Simon Savage from a friend's woodland garden in the Czech Republic in 2002.

'E.A. Bowles'

Price	€€
Blooming time	Late
Vigour	

A snowdrop of superlatives, 'E.A. Bowles' is the epitome of showiness: Very tall with huge pure white and perfectly poculiform flowers, this magnificent snowdrop shows up from a long distance. The effect is enhanced by the fact that two flower scapes are usually produced per (enormous) bulb. On secondary flowers some of the segments may be slightly deformed – a flaw hardly noticable. The broad plicate leaves typical of *Galanthus plicatus* harmonise with the flowers and are equally attractive. Michael Myers found this snowdrop in E.A. Bowles' garden at Myddleton House in 2002.

'Ecusson d'Or'

Price	€€
Blooming time	Main Season
Vigour	

What a story! Travelling in a friend's car near the hamlet of Ecusson in Normandy in 2002, Mark Brown spotted three clumps of this yellow snowdrop in a roadside ditch. Can you hear Mark's yell "Stop the car!"? The overall golden impression of 'Ecusson d'Or' with its yellow ovary and strong yellow mark on the inner segments is enhanced by a yellow wash – shaped like a blurred heart – on the apical third of the outer segments. 'Ecusson d'Or' is a typical Normandy *Galanthus nivalis* with large curved spathes, which are sometimes enlarged or even split *scharlockii*-like.

'Egret'

Price	€€
Blooming time	Main Season
Vigour	

When the weather warms up, 'Egret' takes flight. Then the slender outer segments of this dainty, narrow-leaved *Galanthus nivalis* lift, the tips curling up. The structure of the outer segments is slightly irregular, making them look frailer and more delicate than they actually are. The mark above the sinus notch of the slim, slightly frilled inner segments is either a delicate V or a couple of green commas.

'Egret' was selected and named by Phil Cornish.

'Emerald Isle'

Price	€€
Blooming time	Main Season
Vigour	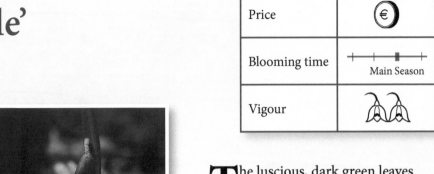

The luscious, dark green leaves of this *Galanthus ikariae* are a welcome sight at the end of winter. 'Emerald Isle' is short of stature, the leaves broad and splayed, while the scapes are upright, holding virescent flowers beneath straight slim spathes. The outer segments are covered in a lined green wash of varying intensity. The inner segments are slightly reflexed at the apex and entirely covered in green, except for the margin. 'Emerald Isle' was discovered by Megan Morris in Co. Limerick (Ireland) in 1986.

'Epiphany'

Price	 €
Blooming time	Early
Vigour	

Everything about this snowdrop emanates slender elegance, from its poise and narrow leaves to the slim ovary and sleek flowers with long-clawed pointed outer segments. The inners are pronouncedly grooved, slightly flared at the apex, and the very small green mark above the tiny sinus notch bleeds slightly towards the base.

Selected and named by David Bromley in reference to its early flowering time, this *Galanthus elwesii var. monostictus* tends to make a later appearance in continental climes.

'Fieldgate Forte'

Price	€
Blooming time	Late
Vigour	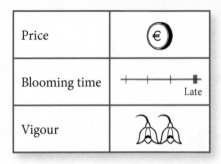

An aptly named hybrid snowdrop, 'Fieldgate Forte' is a tall and substantial plant with upright scapes and thick, inflated spathes. The outer segments display a basal mark and a large apical chevron of a light olive-green colour. The inner segments are evenly dark green, except for the margin and a band of white at the base. Mature bulbs produce two flowers. Oddly, the smaller flower on the shorter scape usually appears well before the main flower. The leaves are widely splayed and have a faint glaucous stripe down the middle.

'Fieldgate Forte' was raised by Colin Mason in the late 1990s.

'Flocon de Neige'

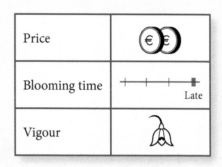

Price	€€
Blooming time	Late
Vigour	

The flowers of this charming little *Galanthus nivalis* double really are reminiscent of a snowflake. Six slim outer segments, which sometimes bear a few green apical lines, spread out to make room for a dense skirt of inner segments. These bear a V-mark, sometimes blurred, and elongate in time. The flowers lift our spirits by remaining open in bad weather – an appealing trait of all double snowdrops.

Mark Brown found 'Flocon de Neige' in the mid 1980s.

'Frank Lebsa'

Price	€€€
Blooming time	Autumn
Vigour	

When the days are shortest and the weather dismal, this superb snowdrop warms the heart. The large olive-green crown on the outer segments of 'Frank Lebsa' extends to the inner surface. More than half of the inner segment is covered by a bold dark green mark. The good-sized flowers of this *Galanthus elwesii var. monostictus* are held well above the foliage by strong scapes. Found in 1999 amongst bulk-*elwesii* by Jörg Lebsa's mother, it was named in memory of his late brother.

'Funny Justine'

Price	$\textcircled{€}$
Blooming time	Main Season
Vigour	

This facetious little snowdrop seems to look up at the sky to check the weather. 'Funny Justine' has pedicels so short, the flower remains upright for a long time, supported by the spathe, before it eventually drops at the end of flowering. The convex outer segments bear a distinct light green apical mark, on the inners the slightly darker mark above the sinus bleeds into an apple green wash towards the base. The scapes and the narrow green leaves of this hybrid snowdrop are upright.

Raised in Belgium by Cathy Portier and named after her delightful youngest daughter.

'Galatea'

Price	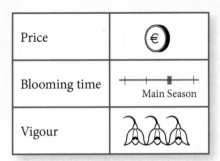
Blooming time	Main Season
Vigour	

There is some discussion about whether the snowdrop (re)introduced by Herbert Ransom in the early 1970s is the same plant as the one bred and named by James Allen in 1891. However, this doesn't diminish the delight that this well proportioned hybrid snowdrop gives when clumps and drifts bring your garden to life at the end of winter. The leaves are glaucous and fairly narrow. Held well above the leaves on long sturdy scapes, the flowers are large and shapely. The V-mark on the inner segments forms a right angle – a foolproof way to distinguish 'Galatea' from 'Magnet'.

'Gloria'

Price	€
Blooming time	Main Season
Vigour	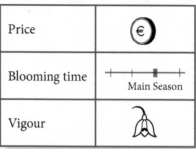

The semi-poculiform flowers of this *Galanthus nivalis* are quite sizable compared to its smallish stature. The inner segments retain their sinus notch and are elegantly elongated, yet do not quite match the outers. Occasionally there is tiny slither of green as a remnant of the inner mark. Like many semi-poculiform *G. nivalis* from Normandy 'Gloria' has a long flowering season. It was found by Mark Brown near Les Jardins d'Angelique, named after their creator Gloria Lebellegard and introduced around 2010.

'Godfrey Owen'

Price	€
Blooming time	Early
Vigour	

This exceptionally beautiful, short *Galanthus elwesii* has become a much loved classic since it was introduced 20 years ago. It is unusual in having 6 outer and 6 short inner segments, which are only glimpsed at the end of flowering. Seen from above, the outers spread out to form a star in warmer weather. The mark on the inners varies and can consist of two apical dots or a narrow V and two basal smudges. Sometimes these marks are joined to form an X. 'Godfrey Owen', which seems to do best in rich soil, was found around 1996 by Margaret Owen, who named it after her husband.

'Golden Chalice'

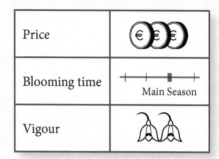

Price	
Blooming time	Main Season
Vigour	

For years there were rumours about this gorgeous yellow snowdrop, a seedling bred by Jörg Lebsa. When I first saw it in his beautiful garden near Leipzig in 2019, I was quite smitten. Both outer and inner segments of the inverse poculiform flower are thickly textured and lined. The glowing yellow apical mark forms a broad V on both segments, diffusing into a delicate golden wash towards the base. More gold covers the inner surfaces of both inner and outer segments. The ovary, pedicel and strong upright scapes of 'Golden Chalice' are green, adding contrast and charm.

'Golden Fleece'

Price	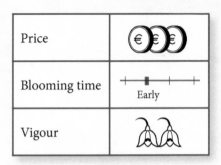
Blooming time	Early
Vigour	

When he introduced it in 2014, it had taken Joe Sharman of Monksilver Nursery more than 10 years of breeding effort to achieve this pterugiform (inverse poculiform) yellow *Galanthus plicatus*. While the tips of the explicative leaves, the scapes and pedicels show a yellow tinge, the ovaries are golden and there are strong golden marks on the tips of the outer segments and above the sinus of the inners. In some locations these may be lime-yellow. It is delightful to watch the outer segments elongate and flare increasingly in time. Like other yellow snowdrops 'Golden Fleece' profits from afternoon sunshine.

'Goldfink'

Price	€€€
Blooming time	Late
Vigour	

To see a flock of 'Goldfink' (German for goldfinch) in the garden is a truly wonderful experience. The flower of this fairly short inverse poculiform snowdrop is large and showy, bearing a broad U in a glowing lemony yellow both on the outer and the inner segments. The outer segments are very broad and of a thickly lined texture. Ovary, spathes, upright scapes and leaves are all green. 'Goldfink' is a colour change-hybrid with 'Pumpot' in its parentage.

It was bred by Jörg Lebsa and is still very rare.

'Green Bear'

Price	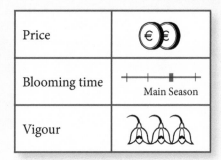
Blooming time	Main Season
Vigour	

A striking poculiform *Galanthus elwesii* from British Columbia, 'Green Bear' is a result of Calvor Palmateer's snowdrop breeding programme. The inner segments have the same pointed boat-shape as the outers and are only slightly shorter. The remnants of the apical mark form two distinct green triangles. 'Green Bear' is typical of several of Calvor's named cultivars, which raise their outer segments in warmer weather while the inners remain pendant. There are often two flowers per bulb, the secondary and smaller flowers appearing later and on shorter scapes. 'Green Bear' was introduced around 2015.

'Green Mile'

Price	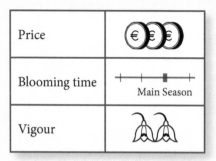
Blooming time	Main Season
Vigour	

Robin Callens from Belgium spotted this snowdrop amongst thousands of white *Galanthus nivalis* and introduced it in 2013. Many collectors consider this big and well proportioned snowdrop the greenest and most beautiful of all virescents. The outer segments are washed in luminous green, leaving only a round white mark at the tips and a white margin. The inners are completely marked in dark green, again edged in white.

'Greenish'

Price	€
Blooming time	Late
Vigour	

Though only of medium size, 'Greenish' carries its flowers well above erect leaves on upright scapes. The outer segments are adorned by green lines that fuse in the middle to produce a delicate green wash between the lines, leaving the base and apex white. On the inner segments a white band along the lower edge contrasts beautifully with the dark patch above the sinus, which extends as a blurred U towards the base, where it forms two darker spots. 'Greenish' was found in 1963 by Fritz Kummert in a wild Austrian population.

'Hagen Hastdunichtgesehn'

Price	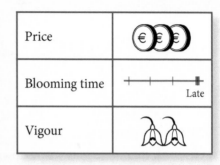
Blooming time	Late
Vigour	

This beautiful virescent *Galanthus nivalis* was spotted by Hagen Engelmann's wife Karla on a Saturday morning patrol of their garden. Hagen himself had walked past it. Karla's cry "Hagen, didn't you see?" became the name of the new discovery. The flower is large and showy. Two thirds of the huge and fairly flat paddle-shaped outer segments are covered in a lined glowing green wash, only leaving the apex and the base white. The colour of the outer segments contrasts beautifully with the neat glaucous leaves. The inner segments are dark green with some lighter green clouding.

'Hans Guck-in-die-Luft'

Price	€̲
Blooming time	Main Season
Vigour	(flowers illustration)

The attractive plicate leaves of 'Hans Guck-in-die-Luft' with their glaucous stripe down the middle bear witness to its *plicatus × elwesii* parentage. The outer segments of this grumpy-faced snowdrop are large and rounded. The slim apical mark on the inner segment is dark green while the eyes near the base are light green. In 2008 Hans Joschko named this attractive and sturdy snowdrop – found by a friend – after a character in a classic German childrens' book. Dreamy Hans Guck-in-die-Luft never looked where he was walking, his eyes always up in the air - until, inadvertently, he stepped off a pier...

'Helen Tomlinson'

Price	€
Blooming time	Main Season
Vigour	(three snowdrop symbols)

Though 'Helen Tomlinson' may not have any outstanding features, this *Galanthus elwesii var. monostictus* has a number of characteristics which make it an excellent garden plant: The shapely flower is large and the outer segments, which may be adorned by a slight green mark on the inner surface, lift up

in warmer weather. The apical edge of the inner segments is frilled. The well defined apical mark above the small sinus notch has a distinctive flattened U-shape and covers about a third of the segment. The handsome leaves of 'Helen Tomlinson' are glaucous with a marked blueish tinge. It was named after John Tomlinson's wife sometime before 2000.

'Helios'

Price	
Blooming time	Main Season
Vigour	

Named for the Greek sun god, this dainty little *Galanthus nivalis* has an overall pale golden glow. The leaves are light green, the upright scapes and short spathes are yellowish green. The typical *nivalis* flowers are topped by a yellow ovary. The pale yellow apical mark on the inner segments is diffuse and divided by the sinus notch. Gert-Jan van der Kolk selected this little beauty in the 2010s.

'Herzilein'

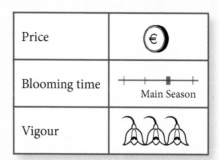

Price	€
Blooming time	Main Season
Vigour	

Around the turn of the century Arthur Winkelmann grew snowdrops from seed sent to him from Russia by a gardener-friend. From these *Galanthus × valentinei* he selected this snowdrop for its astonishing vigour and floriferousness. 'Herzilein' is of medium height, has flared glaucous leaves and usually two scapes per bulb. Below the elongated ovary the boatshaped, long-clawed outer segments display the large, perfectly defined heart on the inners. This prompted Arthur to choose the name 'Herzilein' – which translates as sweetheart.

'Herzilein' is a useful snowdrop for picking a posy on February 14.

'Hoggets Narrow'

Price	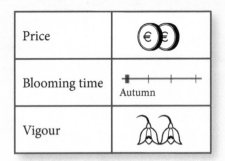
Blooming time	Autumn
Vigour	

Amongst autumn blooming *Galanthus elwesii var. monostictus* 'Hoggets Narrow' really stands out. The narrow and long outer segments combine with a perfect round green heart on the inners and a slim ovary into a snowdrop of distinquished elegance. The scapes are long and upright, their bases wrapped in

typical glaucous *elwesii* leaves which are very short at the time of blooming. Discovered by a group of galanthophiles in the garden of the late Terry Jones, it was named after his house Hoggets and introduced around 2015.

'Horst Kaufmann'

Price	€€
Blooming time	Main Season
Vigour	

This diminutive *Galanthus nivalis* has the typical elongated and split spathes of the *scharlockii* group. The flower itself is almost perfectly poculiform and held on a long pedicel. Both inner and outer segments bear a rich green mark, broadest at the apex and narrowing towards the base. 'Horst Kaufmann' is best appreciated when planted on an elevation.

It was selected by Rudi Bauer and introduced in 2014.

'Ivy Cottage Corporal'

Price	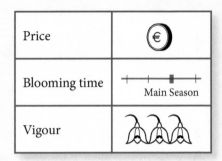
Blooming time	Main Season
Vigour	

The conspicuous marks on the inner segments of this snowdrop, consisting of a dark green apical V and a pair of slightly indistinct basal dashes in a lighter olive green, are reminiscent of the double chevron insignia on a British corporal's uniform. 'Ivy Cottage Corporal' forms floriferous clumps, as there are usually two scapes per bulb. This vigorous hybrid, probably with *nivalis* and *plicatus* ancestry, was introduced by Michael Broadhurst in 2013.

'Jaquenetta'

Price	€ (coin icon)
Blooming time	Main Season
Vigour	(three snowdrop icons)

Starting early in the season with fat flower buds pushing out of the ground, 'Jaquenetta' blooms right through the main season into March. The flower is smallish, rounded and held at an angle by a short pedicel. The tips of the short outer segments are lined in green, the tightly packed inner segments bear a strong green mark.

Raised by Heyrick A. Greatorex in the 1940s 'Jaquenetta' is quite a leafy plant - like all the Greatorex doubles.

'Joe Spotted'

Price	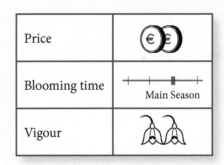
Blooming time	Main Season
Vigour	

Joe Sharman spotted this tall and upright *Galanthus × valentinei* in David Bromley's garden. The spathe is slightly enlarged and inflated. On the outer segments, a large light olive-green apical diamond is complemented by a touch of green at the base. The generous dark green apical mark on the inner segments is slightly diffuse towards the base, where two blurry light green eyes look out at the nosy galanthophile. The long, flaring leaves have a glaucous stripe down the middle.

'Karla Tausendschön'

Price	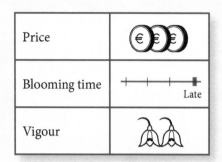 €€€
Blooming time	Late
Vigour	

Apart from its elegant flower, it is the tapered ovary resembling a pointed stocking cap which distinguishes this charming and rare yellow snowdrop from others in the Blonde-Inge-group. The deep yellow apical mark on the ridged inner segments is blurred towards the base and diffuses into a delicate yellow wash covering the whole segment. 'Karla Tausendschön' is smallish of stature but well proportioned, with glaucous prostrate leaves and strong upright scapes. Hagen Engelmann selected this beauty, fittingly naming it after his wife Karla. Tausendschön – the ever beautiful – is the German name for the daisy, *Bellis perennis*.

'Kencot Ivy'

Price	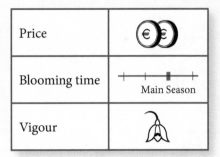
Blooming time	Main Season
Vigour	

When the broad, slightly reflexed and green-tipped outer segments of 'Kencot Ivy' open up, a sulking diva looks out. The inner segments narrow slightly towards the apex. Above the hardly discernable sinus notch a large dark green heart sometimes turns up at the sides to form a pouting mouth.

Towards the base there are a couple of light green blurred eyes. 'Kenkot Ivy' is an upright *Galanthus elwesii* of short stature with long upright spathes and broad glaucous leaves.

It was selected by Joe Sharman in 2005 or 2006.

'Kildare'

Price	€
Blooming time	Main Season
Vigour	

An Irish snowdrop of great elegance and hybrid origin, 'Kildare' is quite unmistakable. The elongated pointed outer segments are marked with green lines that start at the apex, where they sometimes join, and extend more than half way towards the base. The inner segments are beautifully marked in dark green which gradually fades towards the base. The spathe is very straight, the plicate leaves narrow and glaucous, contrasting nicely with the lighter olive-green ovary.

Ruby and David Baker happened on 'Kildare' in 1995, when they lost their way on a snowdrop tour in Ireland.

'Lady Beatrix Stanley'

Price	$€$
Blooming time	Early
Vigour	

An old hybrid double, 'Lady Beatrix Stanley' has stood the test of time. The narrow outer segments have a slight "shoulder" and open up to show a neat petticoat of inner segments. The apical mark is often split into a single comma on either side of the small sinus notch. 'Lady Beatrix Stanley' is of medium stature. The scapes are often slightly bent, the leaves narrow and upright. This pleasing snowdrop probably originated in the garden of Lady Beatrix Stanley, from where her daughter Barbara Buchanan collected it in the 1940s.

'Lapwing'

Price	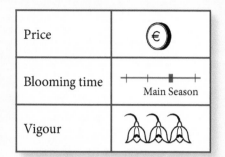
Blooming time	
	Main Season
Vigour	

A snowdrop of hybrid origin that can be recommended wholeheartedly as it is both distinctive and a reliable garden plant. The outer segments are rounded and have a pronounced "claw". They also open up wide in warmer weather to show off the unusual marking on the wide inner segments: a broad green X-shape, the arms angled inwards and paler than the legs. The bluish tinge to the neat and upright glaucous leaves forms a lovely contrast to the flower markings.

'Lapwing' was found by Phil Cornish in 1997 when he lost his way and happend on it in a patch of snowdrops near the village of Lapworth.

'Lord Lieutenant'

Price	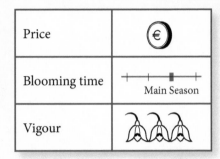 €
Blooming time	Main Season
Vigour	(vigour symbols)

The big rounded flowers of this hybrid snowdrop rise well above the leaves on strong scapes. They are always held out at an angle by short pedicels, giving the impression of standing at attention. The neat leaves have a faint glaucous stripe down the middle. The inner segments are marked by a broad, dark green X that covers almost the entire segment. 'Lord Lieutenant' is a tall snowdrop and an excellent garden plant. It originates from Colesbourne Park, home of Sir Henry and Lady Carolyn Elwes, and was named for the office Sir Henry held for many years.

'Lucy'

Price	€€
Blooming time	Main Season
Vigour	

A tall personable hybrid snowdrop, 'Lucy' has broad plicate leaves and inverse poculiform flowers, held on short pedicels and upright scapes. Mature bulbs produce two flowers, the shorter secondary bloom appearing later. The outer segments bear two dark green splashes, one near the apex, the other closer to the base. The inners are entirely green.

Discovered by Richard Bashford and Valerie Bexley, 'Lucy' was first offered for sale around 2017.

'Medena'

Price	€€€
Blooming time	Main Season
Vigour	

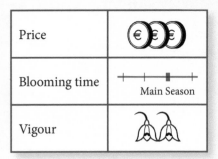

A proud and upright little *Galanthus nivalis* from Croatia, 'Medena' is a well-proportioned and prettily marked snowdrop. The flowers are held on short pedicels beneath curved spathes, the leaves are narrow and upright. The middle of the outer segments is washed in solid light green, leaving apex and base white. The large round apical mark on the inner segments is dark green and slightly blurred towards the base.

'Medena' was selected and named by Angelina Petrisevac about 2015.

'Midas'

Price	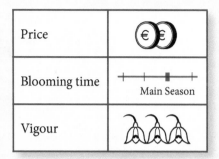
Blooming time	Main Season
Vigour	

This dapper little inverse poculiform snowdrop is a bit of a colour-change snowdrop: particularly when touched by early spring sun (or King Midas) the U marks on the inner and outer segments glow in a beautiful warm golden colour – a pleasing contrast with the green ovary and the spreading leaves with their blueish tinge. But occasionally the marks stubbornly remain lemony green, possibly an effect of bulb size or climate. Thought to be a *Galanthus × valentinei*, 'Midas' was found in the copse at Avon Bulbs in 2011.

'Miss Willmott'

Price	€€
Blooming time	Main Season
Vigour	(vigour symbol)

As quirky as its namesake, 'Miss Willmott' is notable for producing up to 4 scapes per bulb. They are staggered in height though the flowers only differ slightly in size and all bloom at more or less the same time. The outer segments beneath the light green ovary are boat-shaped, pointed and slightly puckered. The apex of the inner segments is reflexed with a slim dark green V above the small sinus notch. Near the base, large blurred eyes of a lighter green look out at the delighted galanthophile.
Ailsa Wilding discovered this hybrid snowdrop in the grounds of Warley Place, the former home of Ellen Wilmott.

'Modern Art'

Price	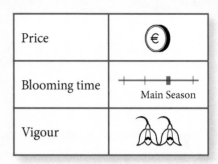 (€)
Blooming time	Main Season
Vigour	

When E.B. Anderson found this hybrid snowdrop in his garden around 1959, he considered it "curious but not beautiful" and therefore felt that 'Modern Art' was a fitting name. However, particularly when the flowers first emerge from the enlarged spathe, it is actually quite handsome! The outer segments are tipped in green and there is an arrowhead of green shading near the base. The large blurred mark on the inners runs up the margins towards the base – but this is quite variable. The leaves are slightly explicative and upright.

'Northern Lights'

Price	€€€
Blooming time	Main Season
Vigour	

A ray of sunshine brings out the luminous quality of the light green, slightly lined wash on the outer segments of this exceptional *Galanthus × valentinei* and makes it stand out amongst its peers. The inner segments are entirely marked in green, which is darkest at the apex, getting lighter towards the base, where it condenses to form two washed out "eyes". The colour of the flower contrasts nicely with bluish green, flared leaves.

'Northern Lights' was found and named by Andy Byfield in 2006.

'Orange Star'

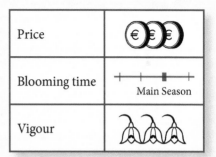

Price	€€€
Blooming time	Main Season
Vigour	

This unique *Galanthus nivalis* has a number of exceptional features: There may be three, four or five narrow outer segments that sometimes bear a hint of green. But most notably, the inner segments are converted to enlarged versions of anthers which, together with the flower form, inspired the the name. The flower of 'Orange Star' is held on short pedicels. The spathe is slightly enlarged and curved, a typical feature of *G. nivalis* from Northern France. Olivier Vico and Ruben Billiet found and named this extraordinary snowdrop which was introduced in 2019.

'Phil Cornish'

Price	€
Blooming time	Main Season
Vigour	

A beautiful inverse poculiform snowdrops of 'Trym' parentage, 'Phil Cornish' is a medium sized *Galanthus plicatus* of upright stature, displaying a range of different greens. Most notably the broad outer segments bear a double mark: a large dark green heart at the apex and a round mark of a paler green at the base. The mark on the inner segment is entirely dark green, fading slightly towards the base. Contrasting with the flower, the leaves are glaucous with a lighter stripe down the middle.

This beauty arose in the garden of Phil Cornish, who eventually agreed to it bearing his name.

'Philippe André Meyer'

Price	 €€
Blooming time	Main Season
Vigour	(vigour symbols)

The flower of this delightful inverse poculiform *G. plicatus*-hybrid resembles that of greatly valued 'South Hayes': a green stripe adornes the outer segments, starting at the base and ending just short of the apex where it broadens into a triangle. The inner segments are completely marked in green, leaving a white ribbon above the sinus notch. 'Philippe André Meyer' has an upright habit and great poise, though it is altogether a little shorter than 'South Hayes'. Found by Mark Brown, who named this snowdrop after his highly respected former employer.

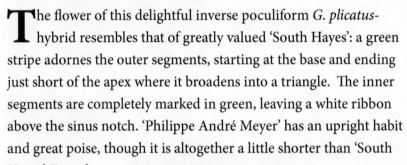

'Poculi Perfect'

Price	(€)
Blooming time	⊢——┼——┼——■ Late
Vigour	(vigour symbol)

This fairly tall *Galanthus nivalis* is aptly named as its flowers are perfectly and uniformly poculiform. All segments are boat-shaped, slightly ridged and perfectly white. The large flowers are carried upright on strong scapes and beautifully offset by long, widely splayed curving leaves that are glaucous and a little wider than usual. 'Poculi Perfect' was found in 2009 by Pavel Sekerka near Melnik in the Czech Republic and named in 2011 by the Latvian bulb specialist Jānis Rukšāns.

'Potters Prelude'

Price	€
Blooming time	Autumn
Vigour	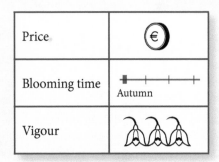

This *Galanthus elwesii var. monostictus* has stood the test of time. Selected in the 1960s by Jack Potter, former curator of the Scott Arboretum in Pennsylvania, it has proven its worth as a robust and reliable garden plant. The flowers are held on upright sturdy scapes, whilst the leaves are very short at flowering. The typically large ovary of 'Potters Prelude' shows hardly any waist at the base of the flower. The outer segments are thickly textured. Covering two thirds of the inners, the apical mark above the pronounced sinus notch resembles a flamboyant heart.

'Ray Cobb'

Price	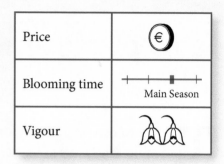
Blooming time	Main Season
Vigour	

I n the right location, where it gets some afternoon sun, 'Ray Cobb' is a superb yellow *Galanthus nivalis*. The ovary and the pedicel as well as the generous apical mark on the inner segments glow golden, while scapes, spathe valves and leaves are green. The history of this snowdrop remains somewhat nebulous, but it was certainly Ray Cobb who first noted it as something special. Therefore, John Foster named it after Ray and introduced it in 1999.

'Ronald Mackenzie'

Price	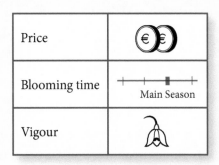 (€€)
Blooming time	Main Season
Vigour	

Aglorious snowdrop that has driven me to distraction – I have lost it three times! But I don't give up on my favourite yellow – which seems to be difficult for other galantahophiles, too. The outer segments have long claws, are wide, rounded and slightly pointed at the apex. The big elongated golden ovary combines beautifully with the extensive and equally golden marks on the inner segments. The shape of the inner segment, with a slightly reflexed and ruffled apex, and the form of the double inner mark are reminiscent of *Galanthus gracilis*. The slightly twisted and fairly broad leaves have explicative margins. This exceptional snowdrop was introduced by Ronald Mackenzie in 2009.

'Rosemary Burnham'

Price	 €€
Blooming time	Main Season
Vigour	

Although this virescent *Galanthus elwesii* is small of stature, a clump of 'Rosemary Burnham' is an impressive sight. Green lines, often joined by a green wash, cover the large rounded outer segments almost entirely. The inner segments, displayed by elongating claws, are almost completely dark green, there is only some white along the base and above the tiny sinus notch. This exceptional Canadian snowdrop, which prefers a bit of shade, was found in the early 1960s by Rosemary Burnham in British Columbia and named for her.

'Ruby's Green Dream'

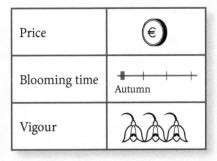

Price	€
Blooming time	Autumn
Vigour	

When the leaves are turning in October, it is a particular joy to see 'Ruby's Green Dream' in the slanting light of autumn. The slender outer segments are well-marked with partly fused green lines, leaving the base and the apex pure white. More than a third of the inner segments is green, leaving a white ribbon at the apex. As is typical of autumn-flowering *Galanthus reginae-olgae*, the leaves are absent at blooming time; they grow over the winter months.
'Ruby's Green Dream' was selected by Joe Sharman, named in honour of Ruby Baker and introduced in 2012.

'Sprite'

Price	€
Blooming time	Main Season
Vigour	

The rounded outer segments of 'Sprite' are adorned with 5 or 6 short light green lines which always start a third of the way up from the apex, as if someone had taken a ruler to them. Two thirds of the inner segments are marked in a very dark fir green. Leaves and scapes of this hybrid snowdrop are upright. 'Sprite' is floriferous and a superb, reliable garden plant.
It was found in the grounds of Avon Bulbs around 2005.

'Standing Tall'

Price	
Blooming time	Early
Vigour	

This hardy and prolific American snowdrop should have a great future as a garden plant. It generally flowers in time for Christmas and happily continues to bloom for weeks. Typical broad glaucous *Galanthus elwesii* leaves wrap around sturdy scapes which – true to its name – stand erect whatever the weather, only bending a little in hard frost. The flowers are large, shapely and of good substance. The inner segments display a dark green, waisted mark reminiscent of goldfish crackers. 'Standing Tall' was selected by horticulturalist and author Charles Cresson. He tested it in his Pennsylvania garden for 25 years before it was introduced by Carolyn Walker in 2013.

'Sutton Courtenay'

Price	€
Blooming time	Early
Vigour	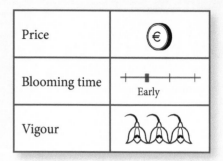

Even in dismal weather 'Sutton Courtenay' with its chartreuse ovary is a cheerful sight. The outer segments of this *Galanthus gracilis*-hybrid are broad and rounded, with claws that elongate as the flower matures, showing off the pretty inner segments. These have a pronounced sinus notch and a dark green apical mark resembling a V with club feet which contrasts beautifully with the light green basal mark. 'Sutton Courtney' produces two flowers per bulb. It is a tall plant with scapes that rise well above the glaucous leaves.

From the garden of Nancy Lindsay at Sutton Courtenay, this snowdrop was first distributed by Primrose Warburg in the 1990s.

'Swan Lake'

Price	€€
Blooming time	Main Season
Vigour	

The flowers of this bonny poculiform *Galanthus nivalis* from Scotland resemble an elegant tutu for the prima ballerina in Swan Lake. All segments of the large flowers are pristine white, of equal length and boat-shaped. The inner segments are slightly narrower than the outers. In warm weather the flowers open up, but the segments are never raised more than 45°. 'Swan Lake' is short in stature with typical narrow *G. nivalis* leaves. It was found and named by Cyril Lafong in 2010.

'The Wizard'

Price	€
Blooming time	Main Season
Vigour	

Tall and upright, 'The Wizard' has semi-poculiform flowers with large flat outer segments. Their rim is slightly reflexed, and they are marked with a green crown towards the apex which is rounded and white. The base is shaded in lighter green. The inner segments are entirely green, apart from a narrow band along the apex. The upright leaves are strongly plicate, suggesting a *Galanthus plicatus* parentage. 'The Wizard' made his appearance in the copse at Avon Bulbs and was introduced in the early 2010s.

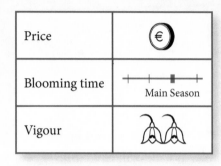

'Three Ships'

Price	€
Blooming time	Early
Vigour	

Will it bloom in time for Christmas? This question troubles many galanthophiles before the holidays, as it is such a joy to decorate the table with a few blooms of 'Three Ships'. The puckered outer segments of this *Galanthus plicatus* expand in time to form billowing spinnaker sails. The inners are flared at the apex and display a goldfish-cracker mark extending almost to the base. 'Three Ships' can suffer from hard frost and is best grown in a sheltered position.

It was found in Henham Park in 1984 by John Morley, who appropriately named it after the traditional Christmas carol.

'Tilebarn Jamie'

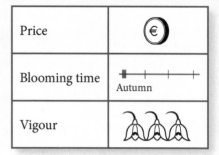

Price	€
Blooming time	Autumn
Vigour	

A flock of 'Tilebarn Jamie' is an impressive sight in autumn. It is enormously floriferous – partly because this *Galanthus reginae-olgae* is vigorous, partly because most bulbs produce two flower scapes. This makes it into an ideal actor when staging a play of succession planting in a layered garden design. 'Tilebarn Jamie' is fairly short in stature, with rounded flowers. The U-mark on the inner segments is slightly blurred towards the base. The leaves develop over the winter months and are narrow with the typical glaucous stripe down the middle. 'Tilebarn Jamie' was introduced in the late 1980s by Peter Moore, who named it for his father.

'Till Sonnenschein'

Price	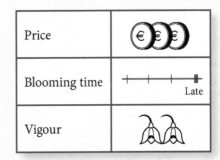 €€€
Blooming time	Late
Vigour	🌱🌱

It is the contrast between different shades of green that makes 'Till Sonnenschein' special. The fairly narrow flared leaves of this *Galanthus nivalis* are of a glaucous blue green colour. Two thirds of the outer segments are covered in a strongly lined golden green wash, leaving the apex white. The apical U mark on the heavily ridged inner segments is dark fir green and slightly blurred on the basal side. It runs up the edges of the inner segments to the base.

'Till Sonnenschein' was selected by Hagen Engelmann and named after his son, Sonnenschein translating to sunshine.

'Trumps'

Price	€
Blooming time	Main Season
Vigour	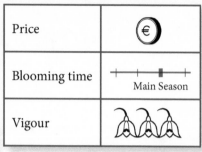

A chance cross between *Galanthus plicatus* 'Trym' and *G. elwesii*, 'Trumps' is the eldest of the 'Trym' offspring. Since its discovery by Matt Bishop in John Morley's garden in 1999, this vigorous inverse poculiform snowdrop has become a classic. The outer segments, which are of good substance and rise up as the claws elongate in time, are marked with narrow green arrow heads. The inners have a bold green mark above the sinus notch with slight green shading above it. Neat upright glaucous leaves add to the beauty of this well proportioned snowdrop.

'Trymlet'

Price	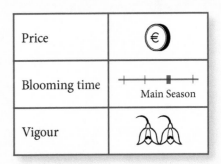 (€)
Blooming time	Main Season
Vigour	

One of the 'Trym' offspring, 'Trymlet' is an upright *Galanthus plicatus* with inverse poculiform flowers. The outer segments hardly reflex and are marked with a midgreen crescent or rounded heart, the inners with a V or U. These marks are paler when 'Trymlet' is grown in a brighter spot. The scapes are long and upright, holding the flowers well above flared plicate leaves. There may be more spectacular 'Trym' offspring around, but 'Trymlet has proven itself as a good garden plant. It was selected by Kathleen Beddington in 1995.

'Valentine's Day'

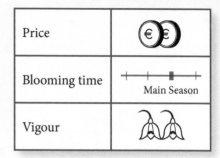

Price	€€
Blooming time	Main Season
Vigour	

Of the numerous inverse poculiform snowdrops in cultivation, 'Valentine's Day' is arguably the most perfect. The outer segments resemble the inners so closely, there is often even a slight notch. The flowers of this *Galanthus nivalis* are of good size and carried proudly on erect scapes. Though smallish in stature, the overall impression is of an upright, well proportioned plant. 'Valentine's Day' was named by Valentin Wijnen in 2004, his wife having found it on Valentine's Day.

'Verdigris'

Price	€€
Blooming time	Main Season
Vigour	

The curved spathe identifies 'Verdigris' as a typical *Galanthus nivalis* from Normandy. It is a tall upright plant with a slim ovary and narrow flowers that give it an elegant air. The outer segments are heavily marked in green. The inner segment markings are a little variable: apart from the dark green apical mark resembling a Kaiser Wilhelm moustache there is a green wash that condenses into a lighter green basal mark.

Found by Alan Street in 2009 while snowdropping in Normandy, it was first named 'Verdure' and renamed in 2014.

'Veronica Cross'

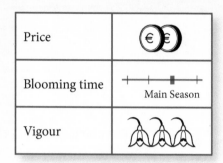

Price	€€
Blooming time	Main Season
Vigour	

A chance cross between *Galanthus gracilis* and *G. plicatus* 'Trym' in the garden of Veronica Cross gave rise to this beautiful and distinct inverse poculiform snowdrop which was named in her honour. The outer segments flare widely as the flower matures. They are double-marked with a dark green apical crown and a light green basal dash, which is sometimes absent. The inners are solidly marked in dark green. Neat upright glaucous leaves complement this dapper snowdrop which was introduced by Avon Bulbs in the mid 2010s.

'Virescens'

Price	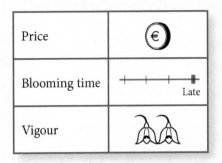 €
Blooming time	Late
Vigour	(snowdrop icons)

This historical Austrian snowdrop, first grown by Eduard Fenzl, director of the Vienna Botanic Garden, in the second half of the 19th century, exerts its charm to the present day. It is the first known virescent snowdrop. The inner segments are entirely marked in dark green, only leaving a narrow band of white at the apex. The outer segments are slightly turned up at the apex and the basal two thirds display a shading of lighter green. In stature 'Virescens' is a typical *Galanthus nivalis*. For me it is quite a leafy plant and the leaves are almost as long as the scapes.

'Viridapice'

Price	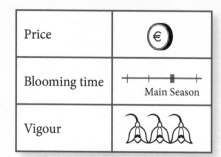 €
Blooming time	Main Season
Vigour	

One of the oldest cultivars still available, *Galanthus nivalis* 'Viridapice' is a showy garden plant, robust and upright in habit. Its flowers, held on long straight pedicels, are conspicuous. Apart from a V-mark on the inner segments there is a large apical mark on the outers which extends – ideally – almost halfway to the base. Typical of 'Viridapice' is the large foliose spathe. It can vary within a clump (and from year to year): usually the valves are inflated, but sometimes they are also split or flattened like a leaf, giving a clump a slightly untidy look.

'Viridapice' was found by J.M.C. Hoog in Northern Holland and first exhibited in 1922.

'Walrus'

You simply have to love this quirky *Galanthus nivalis* double with its variable flower! The name refers to the slim, green-shaded outer segments that grow into ever longer "tusks" as the flower matures. The inner segments, marked with an elongated V, form a slightly irregular splayed rosette. The enlarged, flattened spathe can be curved or upright, and it is sometimes split *scharlockii*-like. 'Walrus' was selected by Oliver Wyatt in the 1960s.

Price	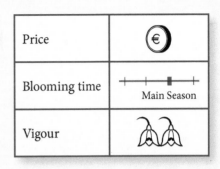
Blooming time	Main Season
Vigour	

'Wasp'

Price	€
Blooming time	Main Season
Vigour	

Aptly named 'Wasp' reminds one of an insect, an impression particularly pronounced when it is seen in a swarm. The outer segments are unusually long and slim, resembling wings, the inners bear a double mark that could be interpreted as the striped body of a wasp. The svelte impression of this hybrid snowdrop is enhanced by leaves that are fittingly slender and upright.

'Wasp' was found and named by Veronica Cross in 1995.

'Wendy's Gold'

Price	 €
Blooming time	Main Season
Vigour	

For many years, among the various yellow *Galanthus plicatus* clones the largest inner segment marking was found in 'Wendy's Gold'. The yellow W with short arms reaches up towards the base, taking up more than two thirds of the inner segment. In some years and some locations (e.g. with little sunlight) this mark may be lime-yellow rather than golden yellow. Leaves and stature are typical *G. plicatus*. As the flowers mature the scapes become a little floppy. 'Wendy's Gold' was found by Bill Clark in 1973 (later rediscovered by Joe Sharman's mother) and named after his wife.

'Wol Staines'

Price	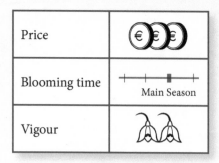 (€)(€)(€)
Blooming time	Main Season
Vigour	

This plicate seedling of 'South Hayes' is subtly and unusually marked: there is a delicate green flush at the base of the outer segments and primary flowers display a little green crown above the apex. This can be reduced to a series of green dots in some flowers. Even in warm sunlight the blooms do not open up much, so one only gets a glimpse of the inner segments. There is a green V above the sinus notch and a large slightly shaded mark above it, both separated by an area of white. Discovered in their garden by Wol and Sue Staines and first offered around 2018.

'Yashmak'

Price	€
Blooming time	Main Season
Vigour	

The marks on the inner segments of *Galanthus elwesii* are enormously variable – and yet 'Yashmak' truly stands out. There are no apical marks on the inner segments, instead there are two blurred yellowish-green "eyes" near the base, which bleed down, sometimes condensing slightly towards the apex. When Ruby and David Baker found this unusual snowdrop in 1998, this reminded them of eyes peeping out from a yashmak veil. In sunlight there seems to be a golden blush on the inner segments, enhanced by the light olive-green of the ovary.

'Yellow Angel'

Price	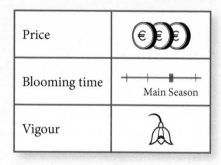
Blooming time	Main Season
Vigour	

This delightful little *Galanthus nivalis* is unusual amongst its yellow peers: Both outer and inner segments of the relatively large flowers are pristine white and entirely unmarked. The ovary is slightly elongated and cobalt-yellow – provided 'Yellow Angel' gets enough sun. A golden hue highlights the short pedicels as well as the scapes which contrast nicely with the glaucous leaves. Richard Bashford and Valerie Bexley selected and named 'Yellow Angel' in 2010.

Contributors

Calkins, Timothy, Virginia, USA: 'Standing Tall' page 83 – all three photos

Bishop, Matt, Dorset, UK: 'Golden Chalice' page 45 – small photo at the top

Engelmann, Hagen, Cottbus, Germany: 'Hagen Hastdunichtgesehn' page 51 – small photos at the top; 'Karla Tausendschön' page 61 – small photo in the middle

Goodenough, Rick, Massachusetts, USA: 'Virescens', page 95 – small photo at the top

Ireland-Jones, Chris, Somerset, UK: 'Ding Dong' page 30 – small photos top and bottom; 'Midas' page 69 – small photo at the top

Lonsdale, John, Pennsylvania, USA: 'Potters Prelude' page 77 – all three photos

Mishustin, Ruslan, Ukraine: hedgehog photo below

Ney, Iris, Waldems, Germany: photos on pages 2/3, 6, 8/9 and 12; 'Cowhouse Green' page 28 – large photo at the bottom; 'E.A. Bowles' page 33 – small photos at the top and in the middle; 'Trumps' page 90 – large photo at the bottom; 'Wasp' page 98 – small photo at the top and large photo at the bottom; page 104

Petrisevac, Angelina, Croatia: 'Medena' page 68 – large photo at the bottom

Seiler, Thomas, Heilbronn, Germany: 'Bertram Anderson' page 19 – small photo in the middle; 'Walrus' page 97 – small photo at the top

Shaw, Stephen, Massachusetts, USA: 'Ding Dong' page 30 – large photo in the middle

Tobin, Paddy, Waterford, Ireland: 'Atkinsii' page 16 – all three photos; 'Galatea' page 42 – large photo at the bottom and small photo at the top

Vico, Olivier, Kortrijk, Belgium: 'Orange Star' page 73 – large photo at the bottom and small photo at the top

Right:
The famous ditch at East Lambrook Manor, part of the cottage garden created by 20th century plantswoman and gardening writer Margery Fish. The ditch is the cradle of several named snowdrops.

Impressum

© 2020 Anne Repnow, Leimen

Publisher: Davidia Press, brand of Prinz 5 GmbH, Augsburg

Layout, Cover and Typesetting: Prinz 5 GmbH, Augsburg

Photos: Anne C. Repnow unless stated otherwise (see Contributors p. 103)

ISBN 978-3-9822446-1-7